Maths Trails
Generalising

Jennifer Piggott Liz Pumfrey

CAMBRIDGE
UNIVERSITY PRESS

CAMBRIDGE UNIVERSITY PRESS
Cambridge, New York, Melbourne, Madrid, Cape Town, Singapore, São Paulo

Cambridge University Press
The Edinburgh Building, Cambridge CB2 2RU, UK

www.cambridge.org
Information on this title: www.cambridge.org/9780521682398

First published 2005

Printed in the United Kingdom at the University Press, Cambridge

A catalogue record for this publication is available from the British Library

ISBN-13 978-0-521-68239-8 paperback
ISBN-10 0-521-68239-8 paperback

ACKNOWLEDGEMENTS
*The problems in this trail were developed by Charlie Gilderdale and
Lyndon Baker, who are members of the NRICH team.*

NRICH is part of the family of activities in the Millennium Mathematics Project
(www.mmp.maths.org) at the University of Cambridge.

Contents

Introduction

Being mathematical has many meanings to many people but some descriptions of what it means to 'be mathematical' might include:

- thinking about and communicating ideas;
- engaging in problem-solving activities;
- creating and identifying mathematical problems within given contexts.

Clearly, these descriptions involve some knowledge of mathematics. However, it is not about the regurgitation of facts or the use of a certain skill (for example, being able to do long multiplication) in a particular context. While both of these last aspects of mathematical knowledge are useful, they are only useful when they help us to solve problems.

So, if much of mathematics is not about learning facts and practising skills, how can we support learners in 'being mathematical'? We need to offer learners the opportunity to pose and explore problems, and to do this we need some guidance and structure upon which we can focus if we are to support problem solving effectively.

The purpose of these *Mathematics Trails* is to help give some meaning to problem solving and be explicit about the skills learners need to develop. In an ideal world perhaps we would incorporate the development of these skills into our 'normal lessons', but first we do need to know what they are and the sorts of situations that open up the opportunities to learn and use them.

All the questions in this book can be used in an appropriate curriculum content context rather than taught in isolation, but the important thing is that there is a journey to make and problem-solving skills with which we need to become familiar. We hope that, after tackling some of these problems, learners will recognise appropriate opportunities to 'generalise' and talk about 'generalising' when those occasions arise in the future. The book will not necessarily make those who use it expert problem solvers, but will help them unravel some of the mysteries we encounter on problem-solving journeys.

Problem solving and mathematical thinking

What is problem solving?

When we are presented with a mathematical problem, it is only a problem if we do not immediately know how to solve it. The process of problem solving is like a journey from a state of not knowing what to do, towards a destination which we hope will be the solution. The key is to have some strategies at our fingertips which will help us to identify a possible route through to a solution. Our mathematical journey is often full of twists and turns where we revisit ideas or need to step back and look for alternatives. Often a mistake or dead-end gives vital clues to the mathematics of the problem and is therefore crucial in the solution process.

To help us identify where we are during problem solving, or what might be a good strategy to try next, it is useful to have a sense of direction. A model for problem solving can help with this. There are many such models but the one below is a good starting point. Although it is written in a linear sequence of activity the reality is a cyclic process often revisiting places on the journey from problem posing to problem solving (see diagram).

Comprehension

- Making sense of the problem, retelling, creating a mental image
- Identifying all the relevant information

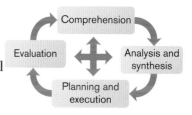

For example, we need to read the question carefully, re-read it several times and/or draw a picture of the problem in order to understand it.

Analysis and synthesis

- Identifying what is unknown and what needs finding
- Identifying and accessing required prerequisite knowledge
- Conjecturing and hypothesising ('What if ... ?')

Planning and execution

- Applying a model to what is known about the problem
- Thinking of ways of finding what is NOT known
- Planning the solution, which might include the consideration of novel approaches or strategies that have worked for similar problems
- Identifying possible mathematical knowledge and skills gaps that may need addressing
- Executing the solution, keeping track of what has been done
- Trying to make sense of any progress made
- Posing new problems
- Communicating results

Evaluation

- Reflection and review of the solution
- Justifying conclusions
- Self-assessment concerning learning and mathematical tools employed
- Thinking about other questions that could now be investigated

When working with pupils this model can help us to talk about what they are doing and help them to set achievable and realistic goals. The model can act as a guideline for questioning or stimulus for discussion:

- 'Can you tell me what you think the problem is about?'
- 'What are you trying to find?'
- 'Have you seen anything like this before and what did you do then?'
- 'Could you have solved this in a different way?'

What is mathematical thinking?

The particular mathematical skills we need to use when problem solving are more than numeric, geometric and algebraic manipulation. They include ideas such as:

- modelling;
- visualising;
- being systematic;
- generalising.

We would class these skills as elements of mathematical thinking that are needed to engage in mathematical problem solving. This book focuses on the skills associated with *generalising*.

The generalising trail

A trail is an organised set of curriculum resources, including teacher notes and pupil hints, designed to develop pupils' mathematical thinking.

There is a large range of mathematical thinking and problem-solving skills we try to encourage in our classrooms. However, it is not so clear how to structure a programme of opportunities that introduce, develop and enhance particular skills. This trail places a particular emphasis on 'generalising' and is designed to meet the needs of pupils between the ages of 10 and 14. The aim of this trail is to encourage pupils to generalise from a variety of problem-solving settings that do not rely heavily on the need for algebraic manipulation. In many standard curriculum documents it is assumed that generalising requires the use of algebra and therefore it is implied that young pupils cannot generalise. This trail is based upon the view that pupils of all ages can generalise and encourages the communication of any generalisation in an appropriate form (which need not involve algebra).

The trail's sense of order and progression (see the diagram on the next page) develops pupils' generalising skills in a systematic way. The aim of the trail is to raise awareness of a toolkit of ideas that pupils (and teachers) can turn to and use in a range of problem-solving contexts. The trail's structure is designed to equip pupils with this valuable toolkit. There is no such thing as a mechanistic approach to 'generalising'. There are no step-by-step rules that will always lead to a solution but, after working on this trail, pupils should feel more confident to generalise mathematically.

Indications of prerequisite mathematical knowledge, links to standard curriculum documents and assessment guidelines are also included to help place the trail within current curriculum frameworks. This gives teachers the flexibility to look at particular problems as appropriate to their pupils' current needs.

The generalising trail structure

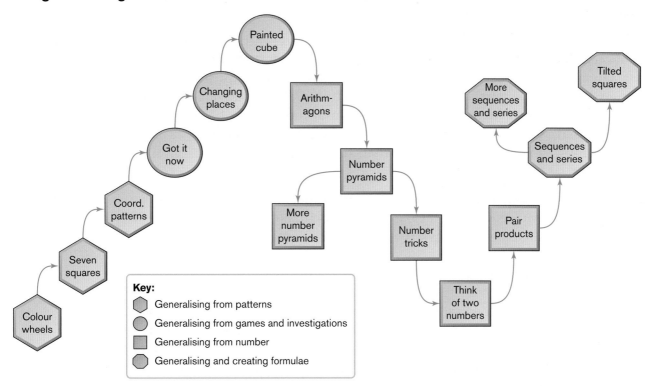

The trail runs from bottom left to top right. In general a problem which is further right and coded with the same shape requires higher proficiency in generalising or involves some aspect of mathematics associated with a higher level of maturity.

Why use this generalising trail?

Pupils may have already met mathematical ideas such as:

- factors and multiples;
- coordinate systems;
- areas of squares;
- Pythagoras' theorem.

They may have used these ideas in different places and at different times in school or at home. In doing so, they will often have had to apply some generality. That is, they will have taken the underlying principle of an idea and applied it in contexts frequently far removed from their original experience.

On such journeys pupils may have searched and perhaps found repeating patterns, perhaps noticed similar features and perhaps spotted a distinct level of sameness about what they do. The subsequent expression of any sameness is the first step towards generality.

Often pupils only experience the applying of formulae and do not experience the satisfaction of understanding them sufficiently to feel confident about applying them in unfamiliar contexts. This deeper understanding reflects the fuller process of being able to generalise ideas and it comes from exploring, applying and explaining the underpinning mathematics.

This resource is an attempt to develop an understanding of this underlying but important journey to generalising in mathematics.

- Generalising is an important process in doing mathematics.
- Generality lies at the heart of mathematics.

- Generalising is not simply about the manipulation of mathematical rules or algebraic expressions.

Every problem pupils will experience in this journey starts with a particular idea or notion and is concerned with pupils exploring the idea further. In doing so we want pupils to rigorously search for similar features and any instances of sameness that can be pursued by them. Through this, their emerging ideas and thoughts about the amount of sameness within a context will be formulated and expressed, and possibly refined as further discussion ensues. The hope is that pupils will conjecture about what they see and test out all their observations.

Conjecturing is not always easy, mistakes can be made, and misconceptions can arise. But these incidences can also provide stimulating distractions on the journey to understanding and help strengthen foundations.

How to use the generalising trail

You might wish to use the trail as a 'course' for pupils over a short or long period of time, working as a whole class, or in small groups or individually. The trail indicates an ordering of the materials to support each pupil's developing skills. However, it is also possible to dip in and out of the materials. The trail has a simple ordering of problems. Several of the problems have a number of similar activities and extensions contained within them but two of them ('Number pyramids' and 'Sequences and series') have a distinct but connected extension activity shown separately on the map above. The trail is intended to illustrate aspects of generalising arising from different types of contexts including patterns, number and games as well as a developmental pathway for improving generalising skills. It is not intended to be a straitjacket. The timings indicated in the teacher notes for each problem are a guide as the intention is to encourage extension and pupil investigation beyond what is made explicit.

The problems offer opportunities for pupils of a wide age and ability range, and do not imply a particular view of classroom organisation. However, there is an underlying message concerning classroom practice and the learning of mathematics as a collaborative experience, valuing the journey through a problem rather than just the answer. While there is no need to offer group-work opportunities there is an underpinning expectation that pupils will be given opportunities to talk about their mathematical experiences *en route* as well as at the 'conclusion' of their studies.

Ideas for managing generalising sessions

The lesson notes included in this book are intended purely as a guide. As indicated in what follows, there are as many approaches to teaching as there are pupils in a class! All we can do is seed some ideas without any intention of being prescriptive.

The CD-ROM includes printable copies of problems in pdf format. All problems can be used as OHTs (overhead transparencies) if appropriate. However, where a problem would benefit from a slightly different layout as a whole-class teaching resource, we have produced a separate OHT for this purpose. These 'teaching' OHTs and any additional resources are on the CD-ROM.

The following might be a typical whole-class approach to a problem.

Introduce the problem

Give a brief description and perhaps start or model an approach. Then ask pupils to work entirely on their own for five minutes – just giving them time to play and familiarise themselves with the context. At this point it is worth emphasising that pupils are not expected to be working neatly towards a solution but simply finding out what the problem might be about; tell them that after a short time you will stop them and ask them to work with a partner for a further five minutes in order to share what they have discovered. The time spent working individually and in pairs is to identify and share initial ideas that can then be discussed as a whole class. This part of the lesson corresponds to the 'comprehension' phase of the problem-solving process.

Sharing and moving on

Stopping the groups after a further short period of time to share findings and ideas of what the problem is about, offers opportunities for those who have not found a way into the problem to perhaps 'get started' and for the chance to refine and develop ideas as a community. Here it is not enough to 'know how to do it' but to leave room for new ideas and questions to be discussed. This is about valuing the journey, including the cul-de-sacs we may take on the way or the different routes we may take. During this time pupils are beginning to analyse and synthesise the problem.

Planning and execution

After these early discussions pupils need time to investigate the problem and consider possible routes to their solutions. Sharing and iteration of discussions will help to give all a sense of owning the mathematics and ensure that, as far as possible, many different approaches to the problem are considered, not simply 'the answer'.

Evaluation

During this last phase pupils discuss their findings, convincing themselves and their friends that any findings they have or conjectures that they wish to put forward are reasonable. Time spent considering different solutions and their 'efficiency' or 'accessibility' is invaluable in opening up the mathematics and helping pupils to value different approaches.

Working with individual pupils

Trails can also be a useful tool for teachers to use with individual pupils who need the challenge of problem-solving activities. Pupils that quickly grasp the mechanical aspects of mathematics but find it difficult to work on open-ended tasks can be encouraged to tackle some of the problems in the trail. The sense of direction and purpose of the trail, when shared with the pupil(s), can give them the opportunity to build up a repertoire of approaches to such problems, and give them more confidence when confronted with similar activities in the future.

Groups of pupils can often find their own way into problems simply by giving them the context and asking them to:

- identify what the question is about;
- consider strategies for solution;
- plan what they are going to do;
- execute their plans.

One important aim might be to encourage pupils to communicate their findings to others in the class or their teacher, describing the problems they had as well as how they chose their approach and executed their solutions. This communication does not have to take the form of written output but could be verbal or in the form of a poster or presentation.

Finally, encourage the group to answer evaluative questions such as:

- Could we have done this more efficiently?
- What have we learnt that is new?
- Have we met anything like this before and were we able to make connections?
- What additional questions did we come up with and answer while we were working on the problem?
- Are there some questions still to be answered?

Many further examples of problems are available on the NRICH website (www.nrich.maths.org) if you wish to extend any of the work in a particular area of mathematics, or simply to reinforce ideas and skills.

Prerequisite knowledge

There are two aspects to pupils' prerequisite knowledge that need to be considered. Firstly, we need to consider pupils' abilities to tackle problem-solving situations independently. This trail does not assume significant familiarity with applying problem-solving skills (in particular with generalising) and has been designed for both the novice and the experienced learner. As the main purpose of the trail is to support the development of problem solving and mathematical thinking skills, this may mean that, as a teacher, the amount of scaffolding and support you will be offering will decrease as your pupils gain in confidence through the trail.

Secondly, each problem depends upon knowledge of particular aspects of mathematical curriculum content which is detailed in the accompanying notes. For example, the trail starts with 'Colour wheels', which requires some basic knowledge of factors and multiples, and can be used to extend and develop these mathematical concepts.

Assessment

Assessment for learning

The notes and other documentation for each problem aim to support formative and summative assessment opportunities. Sample solutions to all the problems are included to give some guidelines. Where these have been written algebraically it is simply for the purpose of being concise; it is not intended to suggest that the use of algebra is an expected outcome. Edited pupil solutions can be found on the NRICH website (www.nrich.maths.org). The advantage of looking at solutions on the website is that they will give you an idea of what to expect from your pupils.

The key outcome for all of the activities is to develop pupils' skills in generalising from a range of contexts. This is not synonymous with 'doing algebra'. If you are listing curriculum content at the beginning of the lesson, care should be taken not to close down the opportunities for pupils to be creative about the mathematics they use. For example, listing 'Recognise rotational symmetry' may restrict pupils' thinking. We therefore offer a cautionary note that the lesson objectives shared with pupils should not 'reveal' obvious routes to the solution.

A pupil self-assessment sheet is included on the CD-ROM and can be made available to pupils at the end of each problem. This encourages pupils to consider the following aspects:

- **Independence**
  Did you manage to work through to a solution even though you might not have had a clear idea to start with?
  Did you need help from someone who knew what to do?

- **Generalising**
  Did you manage to explain or communicate a pattern that you saw, or idea you had, to someone else?

- **Evaluation**
  If you look back on the problem, can you see other ways you could have tackled it which might, or might not, have been more effective and elegant?

- **New mathematics**
  What new mathematics have you learned by doing this problem?

- **Communicating and justifying**
  Were you able to convince someone else that your solution was correct?

- **Curiosity**
  Can you give an example of anything in the problem that has fired your interest enough to look at ideas not included in the question itself?

Listening and questioning are important tools in the process of formative assessment. To support this:

- all problems have suggested prompts for teachers and mentors to use;

- pupils are encouraged to hypothesise and share ideas with fellow pupils, arguing their case – these are ideal opportunities to listen;

- whole group discussions during the lesson can be used to reveal pupils' understanding, misconceptions or lack of awareness of the necessary mathematical knowledge;

- peer assessment can often shed valuable light on the understanding of the assessor as well as the assessed;

- reviewing and reflecting on the lesson outcomes with pupils can help the teacher make judgements and also be used by pupils as an opportunity for self or peer assessment.

As highlighted earlier, much of the work and learning is about the journey through each problem. It is not necessary for pupils to have well-rounded, written solutions for sound assessment judgements to be made. While feedback through marking is sometimes appropriate, oral and continuous feedback throughout the problem-solving process is just as valuable.

'To be effective feedback should cause thinking to take place'
(*Assessment for learning in everyday lessons*, DfES, 2004).

Assessing learning over the whole trail

This section considers the possible outcomes of completing the whole trail for assessment purposes. In particular this trail was designed to widen and deepen pupils' ability to generalise in a range of contexts from:

- number;
- patterns;
- games and investigations.

Pupils and teachers have the opportunity to assess what learning has taken place after each of the problems (see pupil assessment sheet). Here are some concluding points to help with the assessment process over the whole of the trail.

Pupils should look back over this trail and think about what they have been doing and therefore identify:

- mathematical facts they have used;
- the range of mathematical skills they have employed;
- some thinking and problem-solving skills they have developed;
- instances where they were able to be independent – and find things out for themselves;
- places where they have compared ideas or methods and evaluated their choice;
- times when they have asked themselves 'what if … ? what if not … ?' questions;
- other relevant questions to ask themselves and others;
- things that have fired their curiosity – and got them to ask more questions;
- where they have persevered and not been frightened by 'complicated work';
- places where they have found symbols and/or algebra useful.

Links to the mathematics curriculum

The Key Stage 3 Framework for teaching mathematics states:

> 'Thinking skills underpin using and applying mathematics and the broad strands of problem solving, communication and reasoning. Well-chosen mathematical activities will develop pupils' thinking skills … Used well, this approach can focus pupils' attention on the 'using and applying' or thinking skills that they have used so that they can apply these skills more generally in their mathematics work.'

All the problems in this trail will provide opportunities for pupils to develop their general problem-solving skills, while focusing more specifically on 'generalising'. Where appropriate, explicit links to the 'Solving problems' strand of the Years 5 and 6 Framework, and the 'Using and applying mathematics to solve problems' strand of the Years 7, 8 and 9 Framework are indicated in the table below for each problem. The problems in the trail also utilise and develop aspects of the 'standard' mathematics curriculum, the 5–14 guidelines for Scotland and the NI Programmes of study. These links are also listed.

Problem	Solving problems/Using and applying	Curriculum content	Links to 5–14 guidelines	Links to the NI programmes of study
Colour wheels	Recognise and explain patterns and relationships (Y5/6: 79) Explain a generalised relationship in words (Y5: 80–81) Explain and justify methods and conclusions orally and in writing (Y7: 30–31)	Recognise and extend number sequences (Y5/6: 17) Recognise multiples (Y5/6: 19)	Work with patterns and relationships within and among multiplication tables. (NMM Level C)	Developing processes in mathematics (KS2/3) Patterns, Relationships and Sequences (KS2 a, b) Understanding Number and Number Notation (KS3 a) Patterns, Relationships, Sequences and Generalisations (KS3 a)
Seven squares	Explain a generalised relationship in words (Y5: 81) Suggest extensions to problems, conjecture and generalise; identify exceptional cases or counter-examples (Y7: 32) Explain and justify methods and conclusions orally and in writing (Y7: 30–31)	Mental calculation strategies (Y5: 40–47, 60–65)	Work with patterns and relationships by adding or taking something (NMM Level C)	Developing processes in mathematics (KS2/3) Operations and their Applications (KS2 b)
Coordinate patterns	Present and interpret solutions (Y7: 30–31) Suggest extensions to problems (Y7: 32–35) Explain and justify methods and conclusions orally and in writing (Y7: 30–31)	Coordinates in all four quadrants (Y6: 109, Y7: 218–219) Sequences, functions and graphs (Y7: 144–177) Understand negative numbers as positions on a number line; order, add and subtract positive and negative numbers in context (Y7: 48–51)	Discuss position and movement – use a coordinate system to locate a point on a grid (SPM Level D), in all four quadrants (SPM Level E) Continue and describe more complex sequences (NMM Level D) Add and subtract positive and negative numbers in applications (NMM Level E)	Developing process in mathematics (KS2/3) Patterns, Relationships and Sequences (KS2 a, c) Measures (KS2 g) Number Operations and Applications (KS3 d) Patterns, Relationships, Sequences and Generalisations (KS3 a) Position, Measurement and Direction (KS3 b)
Got it now	Recognise and explain patterns and relationships, generalise and predict (Y5/6: 79) Conjecture and generalise (Y8/9: 32–35) Justify generalisations, arguments or solutions (Y9: 32–35)	Recognise multiples (Y5/6: 19) Consolidate the rapid recall of number facts (Y7: 88–91)	Continue and describe more complex sequences (NMM Level D) Add and subtract mentally (NMM Level C)	Developing processes in mathematics (KS2/3) Operations and their Applications (KS2 a) Understanding Number and Number Notation (KS3 a) Number Operations and Applications (KS3 a)

continued

Problem	Solving problems/Using and applying	Curriculum content	Links to 5–14 guidelines	Links to the NI programmes of study
Changing places	Solve more complex problems by breaking them into smaller steps (Y8/9: 28–29) Represent problems and synthesise information in algebraic, geometric or graphical form (Y8/9: 26–27)	Recognise positions and directions (Y5: 108–109)	Discuss position and movement – create paths on squared paper (SPM Level C) Use and devise simple rules – find a formula for the nth term in a sequence (NMM Level E)	Developing processes in mathematics (KS2/3) Position, Movement and Direction (KS3 b)
Painted cube	Reasoning and generalising about shapes (Y5/6: 76–81) Break problems into smaller steps or tasks (Y9: 28–29) Present a precise reasoned argument using symbols, diagrams and related explanatory text (Y9: 30–31)	Describe and visualise properties of solid shapes (Y6: 102–109) Use cubes and cube roots (Y8: 56–59)	Collect, discuss, make and use 3D and 2D shapes – describe 3D shapes in terms of faces, edges, vertices (SPM Level D) Measure in standard units – find volume by using smaller cubes (NMM Level D) Work with cubes and cube roots (NMM Level F) Use and devise simple rules – write a relationship using a variable (NMM Level E)	Developing processes in mathematics (KS2/3) Patterns, Relationships and Sequences (KS2 b) Exploration of Shape (KS2 b) Understanding Number and Number Notation (KS3 f) Exploration of shapes (KS3 a)
Arithmagons	Conjecture and generalise (Y8/9: 32–35) Represent problems and synthesise information in algebraic, geometric or graphical form (Y8/9: 26–27)	Add and subtract positive and negative integers in context (Y7: 48–51) Construct and solve linear equations selecting and appropriate method (Y8: 122–125) Use efficient methods to add and subtract fractions (Y9: 66–69)	Add and subtract whole numbers and decimals (NMM Level D), positive and negative numbers in applications (NMM Level E), fractions (NMM LEvel F) Recognise and explain simple relationships in words (NMM Level D)	Developing processes in mathematics (KS2/3) Understanding Number and Number Notation (KS2 d) Patterns, Relationships and Sequences (KS2 d) Measures (KS2 g) Number Operations and Applications (KS3 c, d) Algebraic Conventions and Manipulations (KS3 c)

continued

Problem	Solving problems/Using and applying	Curriculum content	Links to 5–14 guidelines	Links to the NI programmes of study
Number pyramids	Reasoning and generalising about numbers (Y5/6: 76–81) Solve word problems and investigate in a range of contexts (Y8: 6–9) Use logical argument to establish the truth of a statement (Y8: 30–31)	Rapid recall of addition and subtraction facts (Y5: 38–39) Mental calculation strategies + and – (Y5/6: 40–47) Simplify or transform algebraic expressions (Y7: 116)	Add and subtract mentally (NMM Level C) Continue and describe sequences – describe patterns using variables (NMM Level E)	Developing processes in mathematics (KS2/3) Patterns, Relationships and Sequences (KS2 d) Operations and their Applications (KS2 a) Number Operations and Applications (KS3 a) Algebraic Conventions and Manipulations (KS3 c)
More number pyramids	Represent problems and synthesise information in algebraic form (Y8/9: 26–27) Suggest extensions to problems, conjecture and generalise; identify exceptional cases or counter examples (Y8: 32–35)	Rapid recall of addition and subtraction facts (Y5: 38–39) Mental calculation strategies + and – (Y5/6: 40–47) Use letter symbols to represent unknown numbers or variables (Y7: 112–113) Construct and solve linear equations selecting an appropriate method (Y8: 122–125)	Add and multiply whole numbers mentally (NMM Level C) Continue and describe sequences – describe patterns using variables (NMM Level E)	Developing processes in mathematics (KS2/3) Patterns, Relationships and Sequences (KS2 d) Operations and their Applications (KS2 a) Number Operations and Applications (KS3 a) Algebraic Conventions and Manipulations (KS3 c) Functions, Formulae, Equations and Inequalities (KS3 a)
Number tricks	Develop from explaining a generalised relationship in words to expressing it in formula using letters as symbols (Y6: 80–81)	Mental calculation strategies (Y5/6: 40–47, 60–65)	Add and subtract and multiply and divide whole numbers mentally (NMM Level D) Use inverse operations (NMM Level E) Use and devise simple rules – write a relationship using a variable (NMM Level E)	Developing processes in mathematics (KS2/3) Operations and their Applications (KS2 a) Number Operations and Applications (KS3 a)

continued

continued

Problem	Solving problems/Using and applying	Curriculum content	Links to 5–14 guidelines	Links to the NI programmes of study
Think of two numbers	Conjecture and generalise (Y8/9: 32–35) Represent problems and synthesise information in algebraic form (Y8/9: 26–27)	Place value (Y5/6: 2–3) Mental calculation strategies (Y5/6: 40–47, 60–65) Use letter symbols to represent unknown numbers or variables (Y7: 112–113)	Add and subtract and multiply and divide whole numbers mentally (NMM Level D) Use and devise simple rules – write a relationship using a variable (NMM Level E)	Developing processes in mathematics (KS2/3) Patterns, Relationships and Sequences (KS2 d) Understanding Number and Number Notation (KS3 b) Number Operations and Applications (KS3 a) Functions, Formulae, Equations and Inequalities (KS3 a)
Pair products	Conjecture and generalise (Y8/9: 32–35) Represent problems and synthesise information in algebraic form (Y8/9: 26–27)	Recognise and extend number sequences (Y5/6: 16–17) Simplify or transform algebraic expressions (Y9: 116–121) Expand the product of two linear expressions (Y9: 116–121) NC – KS4 2.5b, c.	Use and devise simple rules – write a relationship using a variable (NMM Level E) Generalisation outside the range of 5–14 (expanding brackets)	Developing processes in mathematics (KS2/3) Patterns, Relationships and Sequences (KS2 a, d) Patterns, Relationships, Sequences and Generalisations (KS3 a) Algebraic Conventions and Manupulations (KS3 c)
Sequences and series	Conjecture and generalise (Y8/9: 32–35) Represent problems and synthesise information in algebraic form (Y8/9: 26–27)	Recognise and extend number sequences (Y5/6: 16–17) Describe and visualise properties of solid shapes (Y6: 102–109) Recognise the first few triangular numbers (Y7: 56–59) Use letter symbols to represent unknown numbers or variables (Y7: 112–113) Deduce properties of the sequences of triangular and square numbers from spatial patterns (Y9: 154–9) Use systematic trial and improvement methods and ICT tools to find approximate solutions to non-linear equations (Y9: 132–5)	Continue and describe sequences involving triangular numbers (NMM Level E) Use and devise simple rules – write a relationship using a variable (NMM Level E)	Developing processes in mathematics (KS2/3) Patterns, Relationships and Sequences (KS2 a, c, d) Exploration of Shape (KS2 b) Patterns, Relationships, Sequences, and Generalisations (KS3 a, f) Functions, Formulae, Equations and Inequalities (KS3 a)

Problem	Solving problems/Using and applying	Curriculum content	Links to 5–14 guidelines	Links to the NI programmes of study
More sequences and series	Conjecture and generalise (Y8/9: 32–35) Represent problems and synthesise information in algebraic form (Y8/9: 26–27)	Recognise and extend number sequences (Y5/6: 16–17) Describe and visualise properties of solid shapes (Y6: 102–109) Recognise the first few triangular numbers and squares of numbers to at least 12 × 12 (Y7: 56–59) Use letter symbols to represent unknown numbers or variables (Y7: 112–113) Deduce properties of the sequences of triangular and square numbers from spatial patterns (Y9: 154–159)	Use and devise simple rules – find a formula for the nth term in a sequence (NMM Level E) Continue and describe sequences involving square numbers (NMM Level E)	Developing processes in mathematics (KS2/3) Patterns, Relationships and Sequences (KS2 a, c, d) Exploration of Shape (KS2 b) Patterns, Relationships, Sequences and Generalisations (KS3 a) Functions, Formulae, Equations and Inequalities (KS3 a)
Tilted squares	Conjecture and generalise (Y8/9: 32–35) Represent problems and synthesise information in algebraic form (Y8/9: 26–27)	Know squares of numbers to at least 10 × 10 (Y5: 20–21) Recognise properties of squares (Y5: 102–102) Know and use formula for area of a rectangle (Y7: 234–237) Use formula for area of a triangle (Y8: 234–237)	Measure in standard units – find areas of squares and right angled triangles by counting squares (NMM Level D) Use and devise simple rules – find a formula for the nth term in a sequence (NMM Level E)	Developing processes in mathematics (KS2/3) Patterns, Relationships and Sequences (KS2 c) Operations and their Applications (KS2 a) Operations and Applications (KS3 a) Exploration of Shape (KS3 c) Measures (KS3 j)

Colour wheels

Generalising from patterns

Prerequisite knowledge
- Simple factors
- Multiples

Why do this problem?
It demonstrates the power of using mathematical knowledge to predict and explain patterns in a visual context that is not immediately obvious as mathematical.

Time
One lesson

Resources
CD-ROM: pupil worksheet

NRICH website (optional): www.nrich.maths.org, April 2004, 'Colour wheels' (includes simple animations that can help pupils to visualise the sequences)

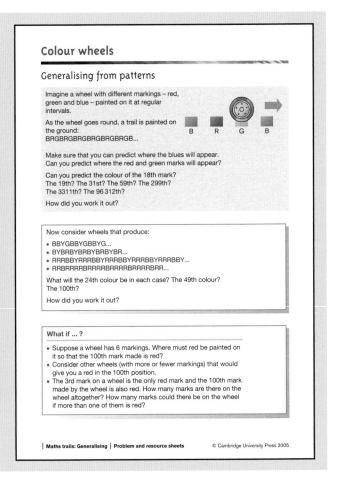

Colour wheels

Generalising from patterns

Imagine a wheel with different markings – red, green and blue – painted on it at regular intervals.

As the wheel goes round, a trail is painted on the ground:
BRGBRGBRGBRGBRGBRGB...

Make sure that you can predict where the blues will appear. Can you predict where the red and green marks will appear?

Can you predict the colour of the 18th mark? The 19th? The 31st? The 59th? The 299th? The 3311th? The 96 312th?

How did you work it out?

Now consider wheels that produce:
- BBYGBBYGBBYG...
- BYBRBYBRBYBRBYBR...
- RRRBBYRRRBBYRRRBBYRRRBBYRRRBBY...
- RRBRRRRBRRRRBRRRRBRRRRBRR...

What will the 24th colour be in each case? The 49th colour? The 100th?

How did you work it out?

What if ... ?

- Suppose a wheel has 6 markings. Where must red be painted on it so that the 100th mark made is red?
- Consider other wheels (with more or fewer markings) that would give you a red in the 100th position.
- The 3rd mark on a wheel is the only red mark and the 100th mark made by the wheel is also red. How many marks are there on the wheel altogether? How many marks could there be on the wheel if more than one of them is red?

| Maths trails: Generalising | Problem and resource sheets   © Cambridge University Press 2005

Introducing the problem

Modelling the creation of colours can be achieved by using a circular disc with colours marked on its circumference. Ask pupils to close their eyes and imagine a wheel which produces a similar pattern and then describe or draw on whiteboards what they see.

Main part of the lesson

After doing the first sequence as a group encourage pupils to work in pairs or small groups on the rest of the problem.

Encourage pupils to:

- build up ideas by describing what they see – 'Can you continue the pattern of colours?'
- model the wheel either physically or by visualising, using a number line to see where each of the colours appears – 'What colour is the number 4? What other numbers are red?'

- look for patterns and note where the repeats occur – 'How often is there a red mark?'
- build upon their notion of multiples and divisibility – 'Can you describe anything that is the same about the "blue" numbers?'

The 'What if ... ?' questions provide opportunities to extend this problem further.

Plenary

Discuss methods and findings from different groups regarding divisibility and remainders. Did different groups tackle the problems in different ways? Invite pupils to suggest other methods they could have used and/or comment on a method you might have chosen as a teacher problem solver.

Solution notes

For the first wheel, BRGBRGBRG..., the repeating unit is BRG.

The 18th colour will be G, the 19th B, the 31st B, the 59th R, the 299th R, the 3311th R, and the 96312th G.

Multiples of 3 will be G; one less than (or two more than) multiples of 3 will be R; one more than (or two less than) multiples of 3 will be B.

For the second wheel, BBYGBBYGBBYG..., the repeating unit is BBYG.

The 24th colour will be G, the 49th B, and the 100th G.

Multiples of 4 will be G; one or two more than multiples of 4 will be B; three more than multiples of 4 will be Y.

For the third wheel, BYBRBYBRBYBRBYBR..., the repeating unit is BYBR.

The 24th colour will be R, the 49th B, and the 100th R.

Multiples of 4 will be R; one or three more than multiples of 4 will be B; two more than multiples of 4 will be Y.

For the fourth wheel, RRRBBYRRRBBY..., the repeating unit is RRRBBY.

The 24th colour will be Y, the 49th R, and the 100th B.

Multiples of 6 will be Y; one, two or three more than multiples of 6 will be R; four or five more than multiples of 6 will be B.

For the fifth wheel, RRBRRRRBRRRRBRR..., the repeating unit is RRBRR.

The 24th colour will be R, the 49th R, and the 100th R.

Two less than multiples of 5 are B; all the others are R.

What if ... ?

The 4th mark must be red but of course any of the other marks could be red too.

To get a red in the 100th position, find the remainder when 100 is divided by the number of markings and make that position red.

If there is only one red mark on the wheel and the 100th mark made by the wheel is red then the wheel must have 97 markings.

Seven squares

Generalising from patterns

Prerequisite knowledge
- Drawing systematically
- Making comparisons
- Basic properties of a square

Why do this problem?

Although the mathematical knowledge needed to tackle this problem is no more than 'Colour wheels' the context is not quite so easy to visualise and connections are a little less obvious but describing what is seen can help. The important idea here is that seeing the same pattern in different ways can generate the same mathematics. There is no one way that is 'right'.

The problem is a good opportunity to use algebraic symbols to explain the pattern but this is *not* essential. Lots of examples of other similar contexts are included.

Time

One or two lessons

Resources

CD-ROM: pupil worksheet

NRICH website (optional): www.nrich.maths.org, September 2004,

'Seven squares' (animations on the NRICH site show interactive examples of how pupils might have created the first pattern)

Introducing the problem

Display a picture of the seven squares. It is not a good idea to draw the pattern in front of the class because this gives pupils a sense of 'the right way' (which of course there isn't).

Invite pupils to work in pairs, one pupil drawing or creating the pattern while the other pupil watches. The observer then describes in words the method used to their partner and the pair agree on a good way of explaining what they did to the rest of the class.

Ask two pairs, one after the other, to describe their different methods to you so that you can re-create them on the board. The aim is to use contrasting methods to identify a 'notation' for describing and then calculating the number of matches.

For example:

> The pattern could be made by first drawing 1 'down' match followed by 7 'back-to-front Cs'.
>
> Total number of matches:
> $$1 + 3 + 3 + 3 + 3 + 3 + 3 + 3 = 1 + 7 \times 3 = 22$$

Or

> The pattern can be made by first drawing 7 'across' matches then another 7 'across' matches below the first, and finally adding 8 'downs'.
>
> Total number of matches:
> $$7 + 7 + 8 = 7 + 7 + (7 + 1) = 22$$

Ask pupils appropriate questions in order to code what they have drawn. For example: 'What is the significance of the 7?'

Ask the class to code their methods. Those pairs that have created their patterns in the same way as those on the board could think of a different construction method.

Use this work to lead up to:

- Suppose there had been 100 squares – how many matches altogether?
- A million and one squares – how many matches?

Main part of the lesson

Select one or more of the suggested patterns in 'Follow-up activities' on the problem sheet. Ask pupils to work in small groups to create and code the patterns in as many different ways as they can. They should aim to generalise the patterns and give a convincing argument (prove) at the end of the session how they know the number of dots, lines or squares needed to create a pattern of any size.

Plenary

There are two main points to draw out of the plenary session. Firstly, share with pupils what you consider to be well-constructed arguments for the generalisation and why. Secondly, highlight the fact that pupils have produced the same generalisation by taking different routes.

Solution notes

Tom's method

For 7 squares, there are 1 down and 7 inverted Cs, so $1 + (7 \times 3) = 22$ matches.

For 25 squares, there would be 1 down and 25 inverted Cs, so $1 + (25 \times 3) = 76$ matches.

For 100 squares, there are 301 matches in total, i.e. $1 + (100 \times 3)$ matches.

For one million and one squares, there are 3 000 004 matches in total, i.e. $1 + (1\,000\,001 \times 3)$ matches.

When N is the number of squares, downs = 1, inverted Cs = N, so $3N + 1$ matches altogether.

Alan's method

For 7 squares, there are 14 matches along and 8 down, so $(7 \times 2) + (7 + 1) = 22$ matches.

For 25 squares, there would be 50 along and 26 down, so $(25 \times 2) + (25 + 1) = 76$ matches.

For 100 squares, there are 301 matches in total, i.e. $(100 \times 2) + (100 + 1)$ matches.

For one million and one squares, there are 3 000 004 matches in total, i.e. $(1\,000\,001 \times 2) + (1\,000\,001 + 1)$ matches.

When N is the number of squares, alongs = $N \times 2$, downs = $N + 1$, so $3N + 1$ matches altogether.

Ruth's method

For 7 squares, there are 1 square and 6 inverted Cs, so $4 + (6 \times 3) = 22$ matches.

For 25 squares, there would be 1 square and 24 inverted Cs, so $4 + (24 \times 3) = 76$ matches.

For 100 squares, there are 301 matches in total, i.e. $4 + (99 \times 3)$ matches.

For one million and one squares, there are 3 000 004 matches in total, i.e. $4 + (1\,000\,000 \times 3)$.

When N is the number of squares, squares = 1, inverted Cs = $N - 1$, so $3N + 1$ matches altogether.

Follow-up activities

Growing rectangles

Perimeter = $4 + 2N$, where N is the width.

Number of lines needed = $7 + 5(N - 1)$, where N is the width.

T-shapes

Number of small squares = $3N - 2$, where N is the height of the T.

Number of lines needed = $9N - 5$, where N is the height of the T.

L-shapes

Number of small squares = $2N - 1$, where N is the side of the large square.

Perimeter of L-shape = $4N$, where N is the side of the large square.

Squares in squares

Number of white squares = $(\sqrt{N} + 2)^2 - N$, where N is the number of grey squares.

Coordinate patterns

Generalising from patterns

Prerequisite knowledge
- Knowledge of 2-D coordinates in all four quadrants
- Properties of squares
- Properties of isosceles triangles

Why do this problem?

This problem is based on ideas found in the *Coordinate patterns* booklet in the SMP 11–16 series published by Cambridge University Press. It is a wonderful context for using coordinates and appreciating underlying mathematical structures.

The problem encourages pupils to communicate their image of the patterns and how they are generated, to describe what they are doing and the assumptions they are making. The three examples are based on similar but broadening contexts.

Time

One or two lessons

Resources

CD-ROM: pupil worksheet

Coordinate patterns

Generalising from patterns

What are the coordinates of the bottom left-hand vertex of the 15th square?

What are the coordinates of the centre of the 34th square?

Imagine the sequence of squares extending to the left: ..., –2, –1, 0, 1, 2, 3, ...

What are the coordinates of the centre of the –15th square?

What strategies are you using to answer these questions?

What are the coordinates of the top vertex of the 23rd triangle?

What are the coordinates of the top left-hand vertex of the 58th triangle?

What strategies are you using to answer these questions?

| Maths trails: Generalising | Problem and resource sheets   © Cambridge University Press 2005

NRICH website (optional): www.nrich.maths.org, September 2004, 'Coordinate patterns'

Introducing the problem

Show the first diagram to the group. Ask them to describe what they see on the picture and what is happening off the picture.

- Can you see any patterns?
- How far do these patterns extend?
- What do you notice about the x-coordinate of the top right-hand vertex of every square? (bottom left, etc.)
- What about the y-coordinates?
- Can you explain the patterns and predict where the next square will be, and the next, and the next, ... ?

Now extend to the notion of coordinate pairs (x, y).

It is important to draw out pupils' descriptions and explanations of patterns as this will support their work in the main part of the lesson.

Main part of the lesson

Pupils address the questions in the problem, discussing strategies in pairs to feed back to the rest of the group part-way through the lesson. Emphasise that the strategy is often more interesting than the answer! So, for example, one group might notice that the bottom left-hand corner of the first square is at (1, 0) and that each subsequent left-hand corner is 'along 3 and up 1'. From there, they find the 15th left-hand corner and hence the centre of this square. Another group might find the centre of the first square and notice that every subsequent centre can be found by a similar 'stepping' method to the one previously described. (There may only be time for the 'squares' pattern in the first lesson.)

When discussing strategies ask pupils:

- What is a good strategy?
- Did different groups identify different strategies?
- Are different strategies equally valid?
- Are some strategies more 'elegant'?
- Can some pupils visualise particular strategies more easily than others?

Plenary

The key questions to address in the plenary are:

- What strategies are you using to answer the questions?
- Are all strategies equally efficient?
- If you did the problem again, which strategy would you use and why?

Solution notes

Squares

The coordinates of bottom left-hand corner of the 15th square are $(43, 14)$.

The coordinates of centre of the 34th square are $(101, 35)$.

More generally (pupils are not expected to use this notation):

If C_n is the centre of square n, the coordinates of C_n satisfy the equations $x_n = 3n - 1$ and $y_n = n + 1$.

If L_n is the bottom left-hand vertex of square n, the coordinates of L_n satisfy the equations $x_n = 3n - 2$ and $y_n = n - 1$.

Triangles

The coordinates of the vertex of the 23rd triangle are $(90, 10)$.

The coordinates of the top left-hand vertex of the 58th triangle are $(228, 5)$.

If T_n is the top/bottom vertex of triangle n, the coordinates of T_n satisfy the equations

$x_n = 4n - 2$, and $y_n = 10$ when n is odd and $y_n = 0$ when n is even.

If L_n is the leftmost vertex of triangle n, the coordinates of L_n satisfy the equations $x_n = 4n - 4$ and $y_n = 5$.

And more ...

The vertices of triangle 0 are $(-6, 1)$, $(2, 1)$ and $(2, 7)$. All even-numbered triangles are transposed by a multiple of 8 horizontally and 6 vertically.

The vertices of triangle 1 are $(2, 1)$, $(2, 7)$ and $(10, 7)$. All odd-numbered triangles are transposed by a multiple of 8 horizontally and 6 vertically.

The 20th triangle is even and transposed 10 times to the right. Therefore its coordinates are $(-6 + 10 \times 8, 1 + 8 \times 6) = (74, 49)$, $(82, 61)$ and $(82, 67)$.

By the same method the coordinates of triangle -35 can be found by a transposition 18 times to the left, giving $(-142, -107)$, $(-142, -101)$ and $(-134, -101)$.

Got it now

Generalising from games and investigations

Prerequisite knowledge

- Simple mental addition and subtraction
- Knowledge of factors and multiples

Why do this problem?

This problem provides a motivating context which encourages pupils to engage in reasoning about numbers. 'Got it now' demonstrates how knowledge of factors and multiples can lead to powerful generalisations and 'winning the game'.

The game of 'Got it' can be easily adapted so that the arithmetic does not get in the way of the generalising. It is a good idea to familiarise yourself with the game beforehand so that you can play strategically.

Time

One or two lessons

Resources

CD-ROM: pupil worksheet

NRICH website (optional): www.nrich.maths.org, February 2002, 'Got it now' (the interactive version of the game

makes an engaging starting point); a challenging extension or follow-up activity is the game of 'Last biscuit' (October 1998)

Introducing the problem

Explain how to play 'Got it' and play against the class using 23 as the target number and selecting numbers between 1 and 4 inclusive. Invite pupils to decide whether they go first or second. (It might be useful to play strategically so that you win, thereby giving the class an incentive to investigate the mathematics!)

Play a second time against pupils, asking them to try to identify anything you do that they think is relevant.

After the second game, invite pupils to share their thoughts.

- When did it become obvious that you couldn't win?
- Why was it impossible to win at that stage?

- Did you notice any patterns that you think might be significant?

Main part of the lesson

Challenge pupils to play in pairs against each other, recording the game as they see best. Their aim is to find a winning strategy which they will test by playing against you.

After a suitable length of time (e.g. 10 minutes) bring the class together briefly and invite pairs to share anything interesting they have found which might help them to win the game. The following questions may be useful:

- What total do you have to make to guarantee that you will land on the target number on your next move and win?
- Why?

It is worth commenting at this point:

- So, is this *not* a game about 23, but a game about 18? Or is it a game about something else?

The discussion at this stage will help to focus pupils and will give those who are struggling some extra insights. Following this sharing of ideas, give pupils more time to play the game together and develop their strategies further, stopping to ask:

- How can you make sure you can reach that penultimate total? And the one before that? ...
- What number might you want to start with?

When appropriate, ask one pair to play against you so that they can prove they are able to win. Invite them to explain how they knew they would beat you. Ask other pairs to give details of any different strategies.

Finally, get pupils to work out a winning strategy for any target and any range of numbers. You might like to give some examples, including a target which is a multiple of one more than the highest number available to pick.

Plenary

Play against the pupils (or two pairs against each other) with a target number and range of numbers of someone else's choice.

Use this game to highlight the strategies being used, including the decision about who starts.

A challenging extension or follow-up activity is the game of 'Last biscuit' which can also be found on the NRICH site.

Solution notes

To be sure that you hit the target of 23, you must make sure you get to 18.

18 is 5 away from 23, and as your opponent can only choose a number between 1 and 4 inclusive, whatever they pick, you will always be able to win.

Working backwards using the same argument, you must ensure you hit targets of 13, 8 and 3 so that you can guarantee making it to 23. As

the first target is 3 and this is one of the numbers you can choose, you want to go first.

The series of targets can be thought of as stepping stones which must be trodden on to get to the final target number. If the range of numbers to choose from consists of consecutive numbers starting at 1 and going up to n, then the stepping stones will be $n + 1$ apart. If $n + 1$ is a multiple of the target number, then you need to go second to win. If not, you should go first.

Changing places

Generalising from games and investigations

Prerequisite knowledge
- Positional language
- The ability to approach the problem in a systematic way

Why do this problem?
In a similar way to 'Colour wheels', this problem demonstrates the power of mathematical reasoning to predict and explain in a seemingly non-mathematical situation.

Time
One lesson

Resources
It might be useful to have a selection of grid sizes on OHTs and OHT counters for demonstration and discussion purposes.

CD-ROM: pupil worksheet; OHTs of blank grids

NRICH website (optional): www.nrich.maths.org, September 2004, 'Changing places' (includes an interactive version of this problem, including the ability to change the grid size)

Changing places

Generalising from games and investigations

A square grid contains counters with the bottom left-hand square empty. The counter in the top right-hand square is red and the rest are blue. The aim is to slide the red counter from its starting position to the bottom left-hand corner (HOME) in the least number of moves. You may slide a counter into an empty square by moving it only up, down, left or right but not diagonally.

Explore a 4 by 4 array.
How many moves does it take to move the red counter to HOME?
Can you do it in fewer moves?
What is the least number of moves you can do it in?

Try a smaller array.
How many moves does it take to move the red counter to HOME?
Try a larger array.
What is the least number of moves you can do it in?
Have you a strategy for moving down each array?

On which move does the red counter make its first move?
On which moves does the red counter make its other moves?
Can you predict the least number of moves that the red counter makes on the way HOME?
Why is the least number of moves *always* odd?
Can you write a rule that describes what the least number of moves will be for any square array?
Can you explain why your rule works?

| Maths trails: Generalising | Problem and resource sheets   © Cambridge University Press 2005

Introducing the problem

Using a 4 by 4 OHT grid and counters, ask the class to suggest moves.

- What are the possible first moves?
- How many other moves are possible after the first move?

The second question helps the class to see that, although the situation appears very open, it is in fact quite constrained.

Main part of the lesson

Set the class the task of using the grid (in pairs) so that after a short period of time they will be able to suggest the smallest number of moves necessary to complete the activity. Ask the class how they will record their moves in order to be able to feed back.

Some questions you might wish to consider:

- How many moves did you take to move the red counter to HOME?
  What is the least number of moves you can do it in?
- How many moves did you have to make before you could move the red counter for the first time?

The class could then spend time considering different sized arrays – looking for a generalisation that links moves to grid size, first for square grids and/or generally for rectangular grids.

Plenary

The aim of the plenary should be to pull findings together and find ways of representing generalisations and explaining any patterns pupils have discovered. A number of useful questions are on the problem sheet.

For a 4 by 4 array, it is possible to complete the change in 21 moves.

On grids from 2 by 2 to 5 by 5, the results are as follows:

Grid size	Moves
2 by 2	5
3 by 3	13
4 by 4	21
5 by 5	29

This makes it clear that the difference in the number of moves is always 8 – but why?

Imagine a square grid of size n. For the first move of the red counter, it is necessary to slide the counters along to make a space. This requires $(n - 1) + (n - 2) = 2n - 3$ moves of the blue counters.

After this there is a series of repeated moves. The red counter moves every third go, travelling down the diagonal of the array. The red counter moves $n - 2$ squares down and $n - 1$ squares across, making a total of $2n - 3$ moves.

Each time the red moves, two blue counters fill the space, creating a new space for the red. Therefore the total number of moves for the red and blue is $3(2n - 3)$.

Hence, the total number of moves to be made
$$= (2n - 3) + 1 + 3(2n - 3)$$
$$= 2n - 3 + 1 + 6n - 9$$
$$= 8n - 11.$$

Painted cube

Generalising from games and investigations

Prerequisite knowledge
- Properties of a cube
- Knowledge of cube numbers and how they relate to volume

Why do this problem?
This offers a slight twist on a familiar problem through looking at what is *not* painted rather than what is.

The problem gives opportunities to apply knowledge of the properties of a cube, and to use 3-D visualisation and packing skills.

Time
One lesson

Resources
It is useful to have a set of cubes of different dimensions made from smaller interlocking cubes – perhaps two $3 \times 3 \times 3$ cubes (see 'Introducing the problem'). The effect of painting can be achieved by placing coloured stickers on each of the outside faces of the smaller cubes.

CD-ROM: pupil worksheet

Painted cube

Generalising from games and investigations

Imagine a large cube made from 27 smaller red cubes. The large cube is dipped completely into yellow paint.

Take the large cube apart again and complete the first row of this table.

Size of large cube	No. of small cubes with 6 red faces	No. of small cubes with 5 red faces	No. of small cubes with 4 red faces	No. of small cubes with 3 red faces	Total no. of small cubes
$3 \times 3 \times 3$					27
$4 \times 4 \times 4$					
$10 \times 10 \times 10$					
$23 \times 23 \times 23$					

Imagine larger cubes being dipped into the yellow paint. Try to predict how this table would be filled in.

Use linking cubes to test your predictions.

Can you see any patterns in the table?
Can you generalise these patterns?
How are they related to what you see?

What would the results be for an $n \times n \times n$ cube?

| Maths trails: Generalising | Problem and resource sheets   © Cambridge University Press 2005

NRICH website (optional): www.nrich.maths.org, June 2004, 'Painted cube' (includes an animation of dipping a $3 \times 3 \times 3$ cube)

Introducing the problem

Show the pupils a $3 \times 3 \times 3$ cube that has not been painted and discuss its properties. Include questions such as:

- How many small cubes is it made from?
- How many of the small cubes are visible?
- How many faces of how many small cubes are visible?

Ask what would happen if the cube was dipped into a pot of paint. Spend some time talking about the number of faces of the small cubes that will end up in the new colour or stay the same colour.

Show the 'painted' cube to confirm their conjectures or to help pupils in making conjectures of their own.

Main part of the lesson

Ask pupils how they might predict how many unpainted faces there would be in any size of cube. This may involve reminding them of the sorts of questions that you asked for a $3 \times 3 \times 3$ cube and encouraging them towards investigating cubes of different sizes.

The class will then need to work individually or in small groups to collect data and try to establish some rules for very large cubes.

It may be worth pausing pupils' work to emphasise that in the plenary it will not be enough just to have a rule but that pupils will need to be able to explain to the rest of the class why the rule works and how it relates to the cubes.

About 10 minutes before the end of the session ask pupils to spend some time in pairs producing convincing arguments for their findings to share with other members of the class during the plenary.

Plenary

This should focus on the *why*, not the *what*. Pupils may quickly offer solutions and formulae or verbal rules but the aim is to convince others that a rule is right by seeing how it relates to the context. It might be a good idea to choose two or three explanations that can form a classroom display.

An extension to cuboids is also worth considering if there is time.

Solution notes

Size of large cube:	$n \times n \times n$
No. of small cubes with 6 red faces:	$(n-2)^3$
No. of small cubes with 5 red faces:	$6(n-2)^2$
No. of small cubes with 4 red faces:	$12(n-2)$
No. of small cubes with 3 red faces:	8
Total no. of small cubes:	n^3

Arithmagons

Generalising from number

Prerequisite knowledge
- Basic knowledge of directed numbers
- Addition and subtraction of fractions

Why do this problem?

This family of problems involves the exploration of patterns and relationships among numbers forming arithmagons. The aim of the first session is for pupils to recognise that the sum of the two adjacent 'vertex' numbers of a triangular arithmagon equals the number in the middle of the side joining them. Pupils may be able to identify and use simple algebraic techniques to solve triangular arithmagons generally.

The second session focuses on square arithmagons and their particular properties, with the possibility of extension to n-sided arithmagons.

Time

Two or more lessons – it may be worth revisiting this topic over a term or year with different (sided) arithmagons.

Resources

CD-ROM: pupil worksheets 'Arithmagons' and 'Square arithmagons'; OHTs/resource sheets with blank triangular and square arithmagons for teacher demonstration or pupil use

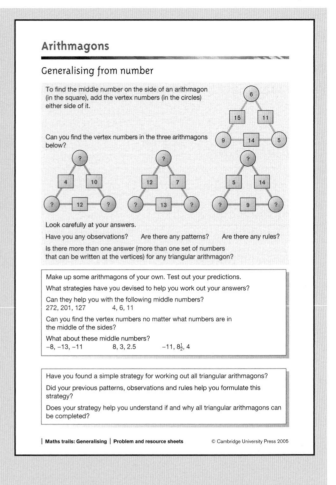

NRICH website (optional): www.nrich.maths.org, March 2005, 'Arithmagons' (includes an interactive tool that enables pupils to explore triangular arithmagons)

Session 1: Introducing the problem

Start with a triangular arithmagon with the numbers in the vertices. Calculate the 'middle' numbers on each side in order to establish the rule in pupils' minds:

> The middle number on each side of the arithmagon is equal to the sum of the two vertex numbers.

Then move to an arithmagon where pupils are given the middle numbers and have to work out the vertex numbers (not so easy). Use the suggested numbers on the problem sheet as the starting point. Pupils will need several minutes for this.

Main part of the lesson

When pupils are beginning to obtain solutions to the three starters, invite them to share their findings.

- Have you all got the same solutions?
- Is there more than one answer?
- Do you notice any patterns?
- Are there any rules?

Ask pupils to make arithmagons of their own in order to test their predictions. The problem sheet suggests some follow-up questions and examples to push their thinking. When they have a theory and have convinced themselves it is always true, ask them to convince a neighbour. When they feel confident ask them to write their theory in a 'conjectures' area of the board or display area. The aim is for pupils to feel they can give a convincing argument to the rest of the class in the plenary session.

Plenary

What rules have pupils found?

What different strategies did they use to find the rules? It is important to share the multiple approaches pupils have adopted.

Can they convince the class (and you) that their rule is always true? Key ideas could be kept on display for reference in the second session.

Session 2: Introducing the problem

Start with a reminder of the findings from the session on triangular arithmagons, referring to the conjectures pupils 'proved'.

Introduce the idea of extending the principles to square arithmagons.

- Do you think square arithmagons will follow the same rules?
- Will they need adapting? If so, how?
- How might you go about testing whether any of the conjectures or versions of the conjectures still hold true?

This should lead to pupils testing their ideas with some square arithmagons. It might be useful to suggest some starting points – that is,

a square arithmagon that works and one that does not. (See the problem sheet 'Square arithmagons' for suggestions.)

Main part of the lesson

Pupils work towards refuting or supporting conjectures they made in the introductory part of the session and coming up with new conjectures which they can share in a similar way to before (convince yourself – convince a friend – prepare to convince the class).

Plenary

The interesting thing here is that the mathematics feels counter-intuitive because what worked for triangular arithmagons does not work in the same way for square arithmagons.

- What is the same and what is different?

Applying the same rules leads to the fact that some square arithmagons have an infinite number of solutions and some have none.

- What are the conditions that make square arithmagons possible?

You might wish to end the session with the following question for pupils to consider:

- Can you extend this to other polygons? Do you think you can find similar rules? For example, will odd-sided arithmagons be like triangular arithmagons and even-sided like square ones?

Solution notes

Some things to notice in triangular arithmagons:

The sum of the middle numbers is twice the sum of the vertex numbers. One middle number plus the opposite vertex number is equal to the sum of the vertex numbers (which is equal to half the sum of the middle numbers).

While it is not intended that pupils at this stage use algebra to write the rule for triangular arithmagons, they should be able write the rule(s) in words.

For square arithmagons:

There is an infinite number of solutions to square arithmagons provided the sums of opposite middle numbers are equal. Otherwise there is no solution.

Number pyramids

Generalising from number

Prerequisite knowledge

- Basic number bonds
- Trying all possibilities systematically
- The idea of maximum and minimum values

Why do this problem?

The problem focuses on identifying a pattern, and from this making reasoned judgements about how to solve a problem – for example, recognising that to obtain a maximum value it is necessary to put the largest numbers in particular positions.

Time

One lesson

Resources

CD-ROM: pupil worksheet; resource sheets of blank four-, five- and six-tier pyramids

NRICH website (optional): www.nrich.maths.org, May 2004, 'Number pyramids' (includes an interactive tool that enables pupils to explore three- and four-tier pyramids)

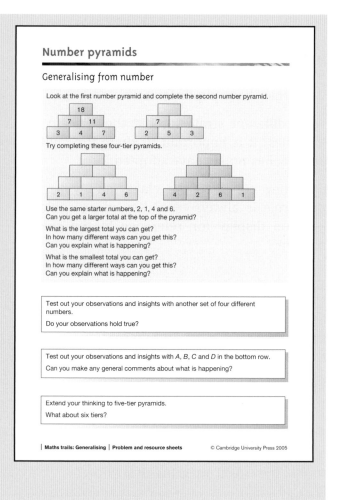

Number pyramids

Generalising from number

Look at the first number pyramid and complete the second number pyramid.

Try completing these four-tier pyramids.

Use the same starter numbers, 2, 1, 4 and 6.
Can you get a larger total at the top of the pyramid?

What is the largest total you can get?
In how many different ways can you get this?
Can you explain what is happening?

What is the smallest total you can get?
In how many different ways can you get this?
Can you explain what is happening?

Test out your observations and insights with another set of four different numbers.
Do your observations hold true?

Test out your observations and insights with A, B, C and D in the bottom row.
Can you make any general comments about what is happening?

Extend your thinking to five-tier pyramids.
What about six tiers?

| Maths trails: Generalising | Problem and resource sheets   © Cambridge University Press 2005

Introducing the problem

Draw a three-tier pyramid on the board and model selecting each pair of numbers, putting their sum in the block above until you reach the vertex. No dialogue is needed at this stage, but use actions in a way that emphasises the pyramid's structure (point at two numbers, then at the 'result' block and put in the sum). This can be done once or twice. Then, selecting another set of three 'base' numbers, invite individual pupils to 'fill in the blanks'.

Working with you and using a four-tier pyramid with base numbers 2, 1, 4 and 6, ask the class to find the top number. Then ask them, on their own or in pairs, to investigate the pyramid by tackling some of the questions on the problem sheet.

Main part of the lesson

Although it is possible to extend this problem to five or more tiers there is a great deal of pattern and structure that can be discovered and shared with the class by concentrating on four-tier pyramids.

Stop after about 15 minutes to discuss some of the observations pupils have made. During the discussion, list questions pupils are posing or develop a question from their observations (such as the following). Share the list with the class to stimulate further work where pupils test and/or explain some of the ideas that have emerged.

- Why do the largest numbers need to be on the inside of the base for the maximum top number and on the outside for the minimum?

- Given base numbers of 1, 2, 4 and 6, what other top numbers are possible?
- What do you notice about the top numbers? (they are all odd)
- The given base numbers were one odd and three even. What would happen if the base numbers were all odd, all even, or two of each?
- How many of each base number are used to make the top number?

Plenary

Pull together some of the answers to the above questions by testing ideas such as the following.

- Using a new set of base numbers, what would you do to make the maximum or minimum top number?
- Can you select four base numbers that are not all even and make an even top number?

It is possible to extend the task for homework to investigate similar questions with pyramids of more layers.

Solution notes

You can get the largest top number by putting the two biggest base numbers in the middle of the pyramid base.

19 is the smallest possible top number with base numbers of 1, 2, 4 and 6.

To get the smallest total, you need to put the two smallest base numbers in the middle of the pyramid base.

Labelling the four base numbers as A, B, C and D, the top number is always $A + 3B + 3C + D$.

Pascal's triangle gives the number of times each of the base numbers is used to obtain the vertex number:

$$\begin{array}{ccccccc} & & & 1 & & & \\ & & 1 & & 1 & & \\ & 1 & & 2 & & 1 & \\ 1 & & 3 & & 3 & & 1 \end{array}$$

and so on.

More number pyramids

Generalising from number

Prerequisite knowledge

- This problem builds on 'Number pyramids'

Prerequisite knowledge

- This problem builds on 'Number pyramids'

Why do this problem?

The main purpose of the problem is to work towards symbolic representation of rules.

Time

One lesson

Resources

CD-ROM: pupil worksheet; resource sheets of blank four-, five- and six-tier pyramids

NRICH website (optional): www.nrich.maths.org, May 2005, 'More number pyramids' (includes an interactive tool that enables pupils to experiment with a four-tier pyramid)

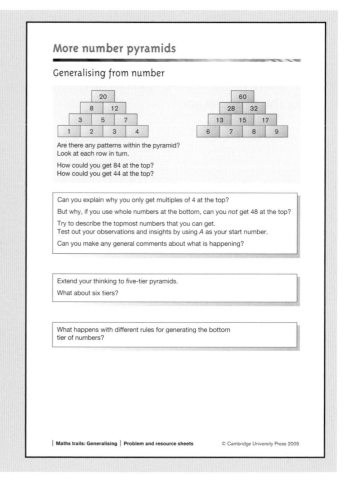

Introducing the problem

Ask pupils to give you a base number to put in the bottom left-hand corner of a four-tier pyramid. Fill in the rest of the bottom tier, adding one each time – do not explain what you are doing.

Model selecting each pair of numbers, putting their sum in the block above until you reach the vertex. Use actions in a way that emphasises the pyramid's structure (point at two numbers, then at the 'result' block and put in the sum). This can be done several times. It is useful to have a number less than 5 and one greater than 10 in two of the examples. Keep each completed pyramid to refer to later. Then draw out the rules involved in creating the pyramid by asking questions such as:

- How was the bottom line created?
- What patterns can you see in the pyramid?
- Will you always get odd numbers in the second row? Why?

- Can you explain why the third and fourth tiers only have even numbers?
- How would the pattern of odd/even numbers change if there were more tiers? Why?

Then, asking for another start number, ask pupils to complete the pyramid with you, explaining the rules they are using and the patterns they see.

Main part of the lesson

Look back at all the pyramids that the class have completed together.

- What numbers are at the top of each of the pyramids we have drawn?
- How can we get 84 at the top? (Referring to the two pyramids you have drawn, one with a number less than 5 and one with a number greater than 10 in the bottom left-hand corner, you could encourage a trial-and-improvement approach to achieving a top number of 84.)

Ask pupils to spend time looking for patterns which might enable them to work backwards from any top number, preferably without applying trial-and-improvement methods. The nice thing about this step is that pupils have the scope to tackle the problem in a way with which they feel most comfortable:

- some might continue with trial and improvement;
- some may notice that they can work backwards using the relationship 'halve +/− one';
- some may be able to achieve a solution using purely algebraic methods.

The problem sheet indicates other routes of enquiry, including considering pyramids with more than four tiers.

Plenary

Ask groups of four to six pupils to select one observation they have made and produce a poster for display to the rest of the class. Groups then go round the class in a circus fashion looking at each other's work.

Solution notes

For 84 the bottom left number is 9.

For 44 the bottom left number is 4.

The use of Pascal's triangle plus the fact that the base numbers are consecutive can yield an algebraic solution. If bottom left corner is A, the top number will be:

$$A + 3(A + 1) + 3(A + 2) + (A + 3) = 8A + 12$$

For a five-tier pyramid, if the bottom left corner is A, the top number will be $16A + 32$.

For a six-tier pyramid, if the bottom left corner is A, the top number will be $32A + 80$.

If you add a constant B instead of 1 to generate the bottom tier, the top number takes a similar form except that the second term will be a multiple of B. For example, a six-tier pyramid will have a top number of $32A + 80B$.

Number tricks

Generalising from number

Prerequisite knowledge
- Mental arithmetic that enables pupils to undertake simple calculations using the four rules applied to one- and two-digit numbers

Why do this problem?
This leads neatly into formal algebra and its magic. Pupils are intrigued and motivated about the certainty that accompanies knowing an underlying structure.

Time
One lesson

Resources
CD-ROM: pupil worksheet; OHTs of the two number tricks

NRICH website (optional): www.nrich.maths.org, May 2004, 'Number tricks' (the two interactive tools can be used as an alternative to the OHTs)

Pupils need mini-whiteboards for the introduction.

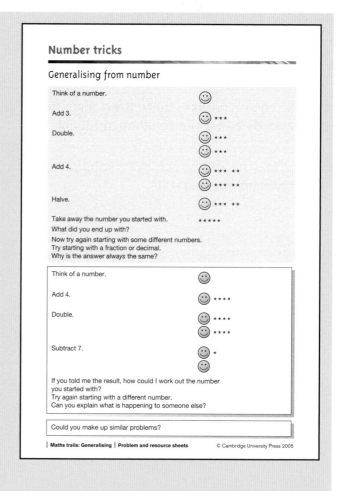

Introducing the problem

Ask pupils to think of a number. Go through the operations of the first number trick using the OHT from the CD-ROM (revealing the steps one by one helps to engage pupils' interest); ask pupils to write their final answer on their whiteboard. (They could use the whiteboard to jot down calculations as they go along.) In revealing their answers, with luck, pupils will notice that they all have the answer 5. Any discrepancies could be discussed and checked to ensure that all pupils understand the process.

Main part of the lesson

Reveal on an OHT each step of the second number trick on the problem sheet. This symbolic form will support pupils' understanding of what is happening.

- What number did we end with?
- Will this always be the case?

Invite pupils to try the number trick again themselves a few times with some different numbers.

When they feel confident, ask them to alter the algorithm in order to end up with an answer of 6. What other totals can they make?

Plenary

Which answers have pupils been able to make by altering the number trick?

Invite one pupil or pair to challenge the rest of the class to find the algorithm for that particular answer.

Solution notes

The answer to the **first trick** is always 5.

When changing the final number, the second addition will always be even and the final number will always be the first added number plus half the second added number. For example, 5 = 3 + half of 4.

In the **second trick**, subtract 1 and halve.

Think of two numbers

Generalising from number

Prerequisite knowledge

- It is useful to have done 'Number tricks' before tackling this problem
- The ability to use some symbolic representation is necessary to take the solution to its full extent

Why do this problem?

This builds on 'Number tricks' because it is about similar structures, but it has an interesting twist at the end (related to the 9 times table).

The mental arithmetic at the start of the session sets the scene without giving the game away.

Time

Up to one lesson

Resources

CD-ROM: pupil worksheet

NRICH website (optional):
www.nrich.maths.org, May 2003, 'Think of two numbers'
Pupils need mini-whiteboards for the main part of the lesson.

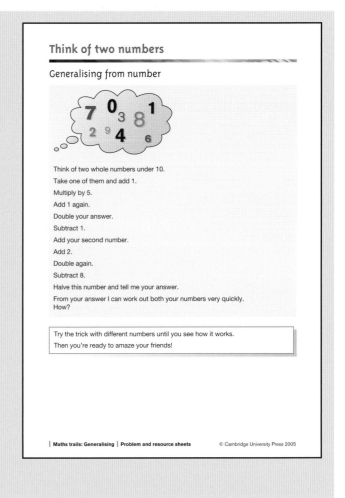

Think of two numbers

Generalising from number

Think of two whole numbers under 10.
Take one of them and add 1.
Multiply by 5.
Add 1 again.
Double your answer.
Subtract 1.
Add your second number.
Add 2.
Double again.
Subtract 8.
Halve this number and tell me your answer.
From your answer I can work out both your numbers very quickly.
How?

Try the trick with different numbers until you see how it works.
Then you're ready to amaze your friends!

| Maths trails: Generalising | Problem and resource sheets   © Cambridge University Press 2005

Introducing the problem

Begin the lesson with some quick-fire mental arithmetic which concentrates on the 9 times table and adding 9 to numbers.

Main part of the lesson

Pupils work in pairs and start by recording their two chosen numbers on one of their whiteboards. Together, they follow your instructions as you go through the operations on the problem sheet and record their final answer on the second whiteboard.

Ask all pairs to reveal their final answer by holding up the appropriate whiteboard.

Impress the class by selecting several pairs and predicting their starting numbers. Pairs can show their starting numbers to the class to verify your prediction. (If arithmetic lets them down, there is a good chance (1 in 4) another pair will have the same final answer and may have got their arithmetic correct!)

Try to elicit from the class the importance of looking at several sets of numbers in order to identify patterns and relationships.

Ask pupils, in groups, to unpick what is happening: suggest that they pool sets of solutions (starting numbers and finishing number), recording sets of three numbers on a large sheet of paper in the middle of the table. It might be useful for more than one pair to try each of the starting numbers as a self-check. While pupils are working, go round the groups and encourage them to write results in a way that will help reveal patterns, e.g. putting the final number underneath the two starting numbers.

There may be opportunities to stop the class to share ideas. At the least, expect pupils to have noticed the relationship between the digits of the final number and the starting numbers (+1/−1). More able pupils may work to a more algebraic solution.

Plenary

Very quickly, pupils should be able to establish the +1/−1 relationship, but why does it occur?

A discussion along the lines that the first number is multiplied by 5 and then by 2, so that it ends up in the tens column, and the second number is multiplied by 2 and then divided by 2, meaning it stays in the units column, will help pupils at least begin to get a feel for what is going on.

Of course, this is not the full algebraic solution, but it may be appropriate to leave it here.

Solution notes

Algebraic manipulation reveals that the final number is $10x + y + 9$, where x and y are the starting numbers.

To find the two digits, you therefore subtract 9 from the answer, and the tens unit is then x and the units digit is y. This is why doing the 9 times table at the beginning of the lesson may be useful, in helping pupils spot that you need to subtract 9 rather than using the +1/−1 method.

Pair products

Generalising from number

Prerequisite knowledge
- The idea of consecutive numbers and how they can be generated from the first number
- Expansion of binomial brackets enables the underlying structure to be represented

Why do this problem?
This is a chance to make use of some standard algebraic manipulation to explain a numerical generalisation.

Time
One lesson

Resources
CD-ROM: pupil worksheet

NRICH website (optional): www.nrich.maths.org, May 2004, 'Pair products'

Calculators should be available so that pupils can try a range of number groups without getting too bogged down with the arithmetic.

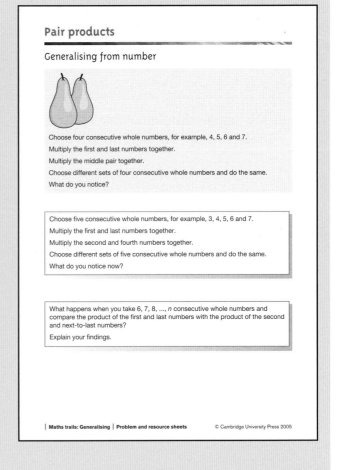

Pair products

Generalising from number

Choose four consecutive whole numbers, for example, 4, 5, 6 and 7.
Multiply the first and last numbers together.
Multiply the middle pair together.
Choose different sets of four consecutive whole numbers and do the same.
What do you notice?

Choose five consecutive whole numbers, for example, 3, 4, 5, 6 and 7.
Multiply the first and last numbers together.
Multiply the second and fourth numbers together.
Choose different sets of five consecutive whole numbers and do the same.
What do you notice now?

What happens when you take 6, 7, 8, ..., n consecutive whole numbers and compare the product of the first and last numbers with the product of the second and next-to-last numbers?
Explain your findings.

| Maths trails: Generalising | Problem and resource sheets   © Cambridge University Press 2005

Introducing the problem

Use a short introduction on consecutive numbers, involving some mental arithmetic:

- Give the next five consecutive numbers after 9999 ...

Move on to the first example on the problem sheet: using 4, 5, 6 and 7, calculate the product of the inner and outer number pairs. Ask for any observations from pupils.

It is difficult to generalise from just one result so suggest pupils try some more sets of four consecutive numbers. At this stage encourage pupils to work individually – this may help all of them to understand the requirements of the problem.

Main part of the lesson

After 5 minutes stop the class to spend some time collating findings on the board without immediately discussing what pupils noticed. This will give pupils who have not had time to do more than one or two examples, or who have not spotted a pattern, to be able to see sufficient data to identify a pattern for themselves.

Ask the class for observations and make a note – this might include a range of ideas. For example:

- 'The products are always even.'
  Is this always the case? Why?
- 'The difference in the two products is always 2.'
  Is this always the case? Why?

Encourage pupils to work on explaining or refuting the theories they have just developed. It may be worth talking about using symbols to express consecutive numbers – this is especially necessary for the second observation (the difference in the two products always being 2) but pupils may be able to explain the first in terms of the sequence of odd and even numbers.

After a reasonable amount of time, working in small groups, pupils may be ready to give a convincing argument for one or more of the rules and why they do or do not work. These findings will need some pulling together and feedback, including some help with representation and confirmation of basic principles.

The last part of the main activity will be extending the ideas as on the problem sheet, with the potential to go even further by considering how the product of the outside pair compares with the product of other pairs. Pupils could work towards displaying one finding with an explanation of why it is or is not true.

Plenary

A pulling together of pupils' findings can be achieved in many ways including:

- pinning the posters up for display;
- choosing one or two groups to share their findings with the rest of the class.

Solution notes

For four consecutive numbers the product of the first and last numbers is always 2 less than the product of the middle two numbers.

Explanation: Suppose the first number is x. Then the second number is $x + 1$, the third is $x + 2$, and the fourth is $x + 3$.

The product of the first and fourth numbers is: $x(x + 3) = x^2 + 3x$.

The product of the second and third numbers is: $(x + 1)(x + 2) = x^2 + 3x + 2$.

So $(x + 1)(x + 2) = x(x + 3) + 2$ for any chosen value of x.

With five consecutive whole numbers the product of the first and last numbers is always 3 less than the product of the second and fourth numbers.

Explanation: Using the same symbols as above, the product of the first and last numbers is: $x(x + 4) = x^2 + 4x$.

The product of the second and fourth numbers is: $(x + 1)(x + 3) = x^2 + 4x + 3$.

So $(x + 1)(x + 3) = x(x + 4) + 3$ for any chosen value of x.

With n consecutive whole numbers the product of the first and last numbers is always $n - 2$ less than the product of the second and penultimate numbers.

Explanation: Using the same symbols as above, the last number (the nth number) will be $x + n - 1$. Thus the penultimate (next-to-last) number will be $x + n - 2$.

The product of the first and last numbers is: $x(x + n - 1) = x^2 + nx - x$.

The product of the second and the penultimate numbers is:
$$(x + 1)(x + n - 2) = x^2 + nx - 2x + x + n - 2$$
$$= x^2 + nx - x + n - 2.$$

So $(x + 1)(x + n - 2) = x(x + n - 1) + n - 2$; that is, the product of the second and penultimate numbers will always exceed the product of the first and last numbers by exactly $n - 2$.

Sequences and series

Generalising and creating formulae

Prerequisite knowledge
- Triangle numbers
- Consecutive numbers

Why do this problem?
It is a good context in which to explore triangle numbers in a way that identifies them as more than just a sequence but also numbers that have some pleasing properties when added.

Time
One lesson

Resources
CD-ROM: pupil worksheet; two sets of triangular arrays cut out from OHTs

NRICH website (optional): www.nrich.maths.org, May 2004, 'Sequences and series'

Using interlocking cubes will help pupils visualise what is happening. For demonstration on an OHP, pairs of triangular arrays with the same triangle number represented as blocks can be turned and overlaid to give an animated effect. An

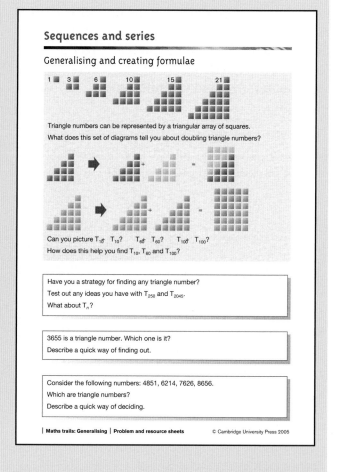

interactive tool is available on the NRICH site which allows a choice of triangle number.

Introducing the problem

Ask the class:

- Why is a triangle number so called?
- Can you make a triangle number with your cubes?
- What triangle numbers can they suggest?
- What is the smallest triangle number? What is the largest? (!)
- What can you say about the product of any two consecutive numbers? (always even)

Main part of the lesson

Introduce the idea of doubling triangle numbers using appropriate resources to demonstrate joining two identical triangle numbers together.

- How did they fit together?

Repeat this process several times. Now introduce pupils to the subscript notation used in the problem.

- Can you imagine $T_{10} + T_{10}$? ...

The aim is to draw out the relationship between the adjacent sides of the rectangle.

Ask the class to work in small groups to find a strategy for working backwards. Some questions to start them off are:

- Given a rectangle, can you find the triangle number that has been doubled?
- Does this work for any rectangle?
- How can you use this to quickly calculate the value of any triangle number?
- Given any number, how could you work out

if it is a triangle number? (it has to be half the product of two consecutive numbers)

At one or two points during the main activity, draw out some of the observations pupils are making in order to:

- share ideas;
- clarify ideas;
- encourage explanation;
- refocus activities.

Assess and reflect on pupils' understanding by asking them whether several numbers you suggest are triangle numbers and how they know. See the problem sheet for suggestions.

Some pupils may say that they can picture them as a staircase; this is a valid response at their level of understanding.

Solution notes

$T_n = \frac{1}{2}n(n + 1)$, which gives:

$T_{10} = 55$
$T_{60} = 1830$
$T_{100} = 5050$
$T_{250} = 31\,375$
$T_{2045} = 2\,092\,035$

Consider 3655. If 3655 is a triangle number, 7310 can be expressed as $n(n + 1)$.

4851 and 7626 are triangle numbers. 6214 and 8656 are not.

More sequences and series

Generalising and creating formulae

Prerequisite knowledge

- Pupils may benefit from tackling the problem 'Sequences and series' before this
- Square numbers
- Consecutive odd numbers

Why do this problem?

It encourages the exploration of the properties of numbers and their inter-relatedness with other sets of numbers. It relates numerical ideas to spatial representation and vice versa.

Time

One lesson

Resources

CD-ROM: pupil worksheet; OHT of grid

NRICH website (optional): www.nrich.maths.org, May 2005, 'More sequences and series'

Counters and an OHT with an appropriately scaled grid or interlocking cubes would be useful for demonstration purposes and may support pupils in their visualisations. An interactive tool is available on the NRICH site which allows a choice of consecutive odd numbers.

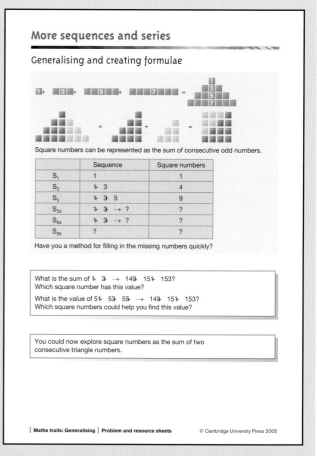

Introducing the problem

Introduce triangle numbers represented as staircases and ask pupils to use this imagery to work out mentally each of the next triangle numbers, perhaps coming to the OHP and creating them with OHP counters or by colouring a grid.

Make a list of the triangle numbers and, without indicating that they are consecutive, take staircase representations of two consecutive triangle numbers, putting them together to make a double staircase.

- What do you notice about this staircase?

Pupils might notice that it is made from odd numbers or even that the two triangle numbers were consecutive. They might notice that the staircase is symmetrical and that, depending on the height of the staircase, the total number of blocks making the staircase is odd or even. If this latter point is raised a discussion of when the total is odd or even may arise. Someone may even notice that the total is a square number.

Of particular interest in the rest of the lesson is the choice of consecutive triangle numbers and their link to the square numbers, so this point can be noted and used in setting the scene for the main part of the lesson.

Main part of the lesson

First step

Ask pupils to work in small groups to:

- create staircases of the triangle numbers and to investigate which pairs of triangle numbers produce double staircases (consecutive ones);

- describe the widths of each tier of the staircases (each layer has an odd number, starting with 1 at the top and then including every odd number up to the odd number represented by the bottom tier).

Can they explain why their findings are always true?

It may be the case that you are asking pupils to confirm their hypothesis from the introduction to the lesson.

Second step – reversing the process

The aim now is to take the notion that any double staircase can be made into a square and that every square number is the sum of all the odd numbers up to $2s + 1$, where s is the side of the square.

Display a double staircase made with cubes or counters and show how it can be broken into two pieces to form a square.

- Is it always the case that a staircase of consecutive odd numbers can be cut once to create a square?
- What is the relationship between the size of the staircase and the size of the square? Can you use this rule to work out the sums of consecutive odd numbers?

Plenary

Encourage pupils to describe a strategy for adding a set of consecutive odd numbers not starting at zero. It is not necessary for them to be able to describe this strategy algebraically. Asking them to sum some consecutive odd numbers together modelling what they are doing with diagrams of staircases may help to consolidate their findings.

Solution notes

The sum of the first n odd numbers is a square number given by $[\frac{1}{2}(n + 1)]^2$.

$S_{25} = 625$

$S_{64} = 4096$

$S_{95} = 9025$

$1 + 3 + \cdots + 151 + 153 = S_{77} = 5929$

$51 + 53 + \cdots + 151 + 153 = S_{77} - S_{25} = 5304$

Tilted squares

Generalising and creating formulae

Prerequisite knowledge
● Areas of rectangles, squares and triangles

Why do this problem?

This problem not only looks at areas and the invariance of a square under rotation but can also lead to pupils establishing Pythagoras' theorem through structured exposure to 'tilted squares'. One of the most important concepts used in this problem is 'what makes a square a square'.

Time

Two lessons

Resources

CD-ROM: pupil worksheet; OHTs of dotty square grid and cut-out coloured squares

NRICH website (optional): www.nrich.maths.org, September 2004, 'Tilted squares' (three interactive tools can support the exploration and discussion throughout the problem-solving process); www.nrich.maths.org, October 2004, 'Square it' (an interactive game that uses tilted squares).

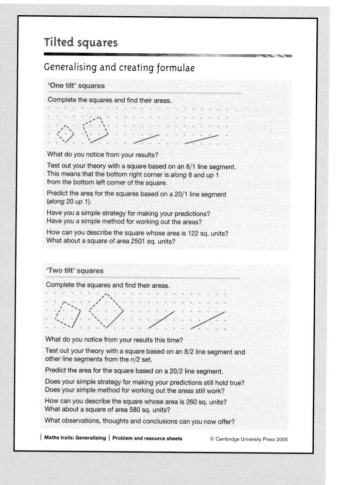

Introducing the problem

The main aim of the introduction is to revisit the properties of a square and consolidate the idea that squares do not have to have vertical and horizontal sides but can be 'tilted'.

Display on an overhead projector a cut-out square from the resource sheet and ask pupils to say what shape it is and why they know it is a square.

Tilt the square and ask them again, confirming that the shape is still a square.

Now place the same square on the dotty square grid so that its base is horizontal and ask again if it is a square. Tilt the square on the grid and discuss the invariance of the properties of the square.

Choose another pre-prepared square that will 'fit'. Place the square on the grid and ask for ideas about how pupils might calculate its area. There may be a number of ideas, including estimation. At some point in this process turn the square so that it 'fits' the grid and lead a discussion about calculating its area:

Area of surrounding square minus area of 4 triangles	=	area of surrounding square minus area of 2 rectangles

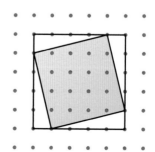

Note: the shaded square would be described as a 4/1 square because the bottom right corner is *along* 4 and *up* 1 from the bottom left corner.

Main part of the lesson

Set pupils the task of trying to find a relationship between the areas of 'one tilt' squares and the amount of tilt (across and up).

After a few minutes stop the class and discuss findings. The area of a 'one tilt' square is $n^2 + 1$, where n is the 'along' measurement.

Ask pupils to suggest a hypothesis for the area of 'two tilt' squares – perhaps $n^2 + 2$. Now ask them to test this hypothesis and establish whether it is true or, if not, what they believe to be true.

Using the problem sheet as a structure, pupils can work towards generalising their findings for squares with any tilt – possibly leading to Pythagoras' theorem.

Plenary

This plenary will need to reflect the variety of levels of outcome that might be expected from pupils of varying ability and experience with problem solving. It is important at this stage to be clear about your core objectives. For example:

- If pupils are to have a secure concept of the 'squareness' of a square then some examples that test this out with a range of tilted squares, rhombi or other quadrilaterals will be sufficient.

- If you hope to reinforce pupils' skills with finding areas of triangles and quadrilaterals such as 'tilted squares' using the concept of complementary areas, then looking at extensions to grid shapes whose area can be found by using a surrounding rectangle would also be a fruitful focus for the plenary.

- The plenary may involve pulling some of the results together, working towards a generalisation for any degree of tilt.

With a very able class some discussion may have taken place during the session as they make progress towards the generalisation, in which case establishing a general rule (Pythagoras' theorem) can then be followed up with applications of the theorem in the subsequent sessions.

Solution notes

Using n for the *along* measurement and m for the *up* measurement:

The area of **'one tilt' squares** is $n^2 + 1$.

The square with area 122 sq. units is a 11/1 square, and that of area 2501 sq. units is a 50/1 square.

The area of **'two tilt' squares** is $n^2 + 4$.

The square with area 260 sq. units is a 16/2 square, and that of area 580 sq. units is a 24/2 square.

The area of **'three tilt' squares** is $n^2 + 9$.

The square with area 153 sq. units is a 12/3 square, and that of area 3145 sq. units is a 56/3 square.

The area of **'m tilt' squares** is $n^2 + m^2$.

Contents of CD-ROM

Problem sheets and resource sheets

Generalising from patterns

- Colour wheels
- Seven squares
- Coordinate patterns

Generalising from games and investigations

- Got it now
- Changing places
  Changing places: blank 2 by 2 and 3 by 3 grids (resource sheet)
  Changing places: blank 4 by 4 grid (resource sheet)
  Changing places: blank 5 by 5 grid (resource sheet)
  Changing places: blank 6 by 6 grid (resource sheet)
- Painted cube

Generalising from number

- Arithmagons
  Square arithmagons
  Arithmagons: blank grids (resource sheet)
  Square arithmagons: blank grids (resource sheet)
- Number pyramids
- More number pyramids
  Number pyramids: blank four-tier pyramids (resource sheet)
  Number pyramids: blank five-tier pyramids (resource sheet)
  Number pyramids: blank six-tier pyramids (resource sheet)
- Number tricks
  Number trick 1 (resource sheet)
  Number trick 2 (resource sheet)
- Think of two numbers
- Pair products

Generalising and creating formulae

- Sequences and series
  Sequences and series: triangular arrays 1 (resource sheet)
  Sequences and series: triangular arrays 2 (resource sheet)
- More sequences and series
  More sequences and series: grid (resource sheet)
- Tilted squares
  Tilted squares: dotty grid (resource sheet)
  Tilted squares for dotty grid (resource sheet)

Self-assessment sheet for pupils